AF326776

Walking into the Sun

Stories from
Classes at the Breema Center

Collected by Jon Schreiber

The Breema Center
Oakland, California

The Breema Center
6076 Claremont Avenue
Oakland, CA 94618

phone: 510.428.0937
email: center@breema.com
website: breema.com

Walking into the Sun: Stories from Classes at the Breema Center

Print ISBN: 978-1-7336310-7-5
eBook ISBN: 978-1-7336310-8-2

Front jacket photograph by:
Vaclav Volrab, used under license from Shutterstock

Back jacket photograph by:
Karen Bilgrai Cohen, used by permission of the photographer

Breema®, Self-Breema® — Breema and Self-Breema are service marks of the Breema Center.

There was a little boy, who, whenever it got cloudy, said, "Oh no! The clouds are covering up the whole sky!"

But his grandfather would tell him, "The sun is always shining—even when you think you're surrounded by clouds—and you're always welcome to walk into the sun."

Contents

Foreword

A wealthy man decided to send the King a gift. He got a jar of the finest rosewater, made from the pure essence of the most beautiful roses. What an exquisite fragrance it had! He poured the rosewater into ten hand-blown bottles, corked each one and wrapped silk cloth around the bottles. Then he laid them on their sides in a silver basket. He sent his most trusted servant to the King with his gift.

The servant was very excited, because he was a great patriot and loved the King, too. He considered this job a real honor. As he traveled to the palace, he thought of meeting the King, and how he would bow to him as he presented the bottles, expressing all his love and respect. But unbeknownst to him, the bumpy coach ride loosened the corks, and the rosewater dripped out of the bottles and evaporated. By the time he reached the palace, not a drop was left.

He presented the bottles to the King. The King opened the empty bottles one by one, turning each one upside down as he uncorked it, to be sure there was really nothing in it. Then he looked at the servant and said, "Thank you."

The servant returned to his master. "Did you deliver the gift?" the master asked.

"Yes I did," the servant said.

"Was the King pleased?" the master asked with anticipation.

"I don't know," the servant answered.

"What do you mean?" asked the master.

"The bottles were empty," the servant told him. "The rosewater must have leaked out, but I didn't know it until the King unwrapped the bottles."

"But this is terrible! Did you explain things to the King?"

"I couldn't. I was told not to speak unless questioned by the King."

"What did the King say?"

"Only 'thank you.'"

One question remains. Do you know how many stories and fairy tales there are where the last part is a question mark and it's left for you to figure it out? There's something important there. Why did the King say "thank you"? Maybe those empty bottles showed him the emptiness of his life and his kingdom. Maybe he said "thank you" because he thought Nature had a different purpose for that rosewater, and it wasn't intended for him. Maybe he knew that if he got the rosewater, he'd have some kind of experience that he didn't really need. There are so many possibilities. And some of them could help lead us to our essential questions.

Introduction

For many years, Malouchek Mooshan offered a comprehensive presentation of Breema's philosophy of harmonious living, Breema bodywork, and Self-Breema exercises at the Breema Center. He often peppered his classes with inspiring parables and stories that communicated one or another aspect of Breema's depth and insight. The stories and sayings in this book are among those I collected as a student in his early classes. I hope you find them as nourishing as I do.

Jon Schreiber

Walking into the Sun

Stories from
Classes at the Breema Center

The Fair Thief

A man went to a wise man and asked, "What should I do for a living?"

"What did your father do?" the wise man asked him.

"My father was a thief."

"You do the same thing," the wise man told him.

The man turned and walked away. As he was leaving, the wise man called out to him, "But remember two things. Be fair. And don't forget your relationship to God."

That night, the man got out of bed. He took a long rope, and some empty sacks, just as his father had done, and set out to find the house of a rich man.

At the first house, up went the rope, and from the roof, the thief climbed down into the bedroom. According to his father, that's where people were most likely to keep their valuables. He spotted the chest, opened it, and found money, jewelry, silver, and gold in abundance. What joy! Silently, he filled his sacks one by one, and made for the door. At the door, he paused. "Wait a minute," he thought. "He told me to be fair. All these sacks, so many…" He put one sack by the door.

When he reached the courtyard, he said to himself, "Is this really fair? Look at how much I've got. What will I do with all of it?" So he left a sack in the courtyard.

As he came to the stairs, a sack fell out of his hand. "Let it stay," he thought, "I don't need it."

As he climbed the stairs, the thought came to him, "There was another bedroom. Maybe other people were sleeping there. That means his family is larger than I thought. I'm one person. Do I need more than all of them?" And he left a sack on the stairs.

He came onto the roof. He relaxed, realizing he had only to climb down the rope to make his escape. Looking down at his hands, he saw he still had two sacks full. "Well," he said to himself, "this is what I'm going to do. I'll share. Half for you, and half for me." And he walked towards the edge of the roof, carrying one sack. Suddenly, he remembered what the wise man had told him. "Oh, my relationship to God!" The thief put the sack down next to him, sank to his knees, and began to pray.

At the very same moment, the rich man woke up. Opening his eyes, he saw his cherry wood chest open and empty. He jumped out of bed, and discovered the sack full of his valuables by the door. Running into the courtyard, he found another sack. And another on the stairs. And on the roof, yet another. Totally perplexed, he turned, and there at the edge of the roof he saw the last sack. Next to it knelt the thief, absorbed in his prayers. The rich man stood there fascinated. The thief continued to pray. Finally, he finished, and reached out to take the sack.

The rich man grabbed him from behind. The thief struggled to escape, but the rich man hung on. "Please let me go," the thief begged.

"First tell me your story," the rich man said. "What kind of thief are you, who leaves his treasures behind? What kind of thief are you, who prays with a devotion I've never seen before?"

The thief told his story. The rich man sat and thought. "Well," he finally said, "let me tell you my story. My daughter is the most beautiful woman in the town. And I am the richest man in town. The most prominent families besiege me with proposals to marry her. But when they speak of love, I don't know whether they love my daughter or my money.

"For years I've wanted to find the right man to be my son-in-law. You are the most fair man I've ever met. But you are still holding a sack of my gold. Be fair. Keep the gold, but marry my daughter!"

Bread, Butter, and Honey

One morning, a boy woke up and went outside and saw his grandfather, sitting on the ground, next to an oven. He was baking bread. The boy came and sat down next to him. His grandfather reached into the oven and pulled out the bread. Then he took a knife out of his pocket, and started spreading butter on the bread.

"This bread is so wonderful," he mused out loud. "Just this morning, your mother ground the wheat into flour and made the dough. The fresh wheat…you know, this land is so beautiful and fragrant. When this bread bakes, it has such an incredible aroma, you can just tell it's going to be delicious." The boy sat there listening to him, watching the butter melt on the bread.

"And the butter—we got from making buttermilk. All our hard work, and here it is, so fresh and sweet and creamy and delicious." The boy's eyes followed intently as his grandfather dipped his knife into the honey jar. "And the honey our bees made, we gathered it. It's from all these sweet flowers, and the strength of the sun, the energy of the sun is in it." The boy leaned towards him, his mouth watering, just thinking about that bread, and butter, and honey. His grandfather took a big bite and said, "Oh my God! Isn't this just *delicious?*"

"How do I know?" the boy said, jumping up. "You didn't give me any to taste!"

"True," his grandfather said, still chewing with relish. "But I *told* you all about it!"

Imagine You're in a Burning Building

A friend came to me with a letter he received. It said, "Imagine you're in a burning building, and there's no chance of escape. What would you want?"

The Scientist

There was a very important scientist, just as famous in his time as Einstein was in his.

One day, he was running through the streets with his hands held together in front of him. One of his friends grabbed him as he ran by, and asked him, "Where are you running?"

"Oh, home to my laboratory," he replied.

"What is it you're carrying?"

"A thought," he said, and ran on.

Riding Two Horses

A wise man used to say, "No matter how good a rider you may be, if you ride two horses at once, either you don't get where you're going, or you get squashed in between them."

The Friend

Nathan was on his way back to work after eating his lunch. He was early, so he stopped at a tea shop for a cup of tea. At the next table a man was sitting alone, watching people pass by in the crowded bazaar. Since they were the only ones sitting by themselves, Nathan got up, went to the other man's table, and said, "Excuse me, may I sit with you?"

"You may," said the man.

Nathan ordered two teas. "Are you from this town?" he asked him.

"I am," he replied.

"We are both alone here. Could I be your friend?"

"You are," he said.

"May I ask your name?"

"My name is Gabriel," replied the stranger.

"Which Gabriel is that, the Archangel of Death?"

"Yes," he said.

"Oh, even though I like you, I don't know if I could be friends with you."

"That depends on you," Gabriel replied.

"If I be friends with you, would you help me when I have to die?"

"What kind of help?"

"You can't leave me here? When it's time for me, you have to take my life?"

"Yes."

"Then I can't ask you…"

"No, you can't."

"Okay. Could you at least tell me ahead of time this is going to happen?"

"Yes," he said. "That I could do."

And based on that, they made a friendship. The more they went here and there and did things together, the more Nathan became fascinated with this new friend of his. He really liked him. And he was so good in his friendship with Gabriel. He never bought something only for himself. Anything he bought, he bought for both of them. If he bought a piece of cake, he got two, and gave one to Gabriel. Always so fun and so good.

Years passed, and then early one morning his friend, Gabriel, came to his room.

"Why are you here?" he asked. "We didn't have any plans. Why are you here?"

"It's time," he said.

"Now?"

"Yes," he said.

"Didn't you promise me you'd tell me ahead of time?"

"Yes," he said, "but I told you many times. Didn't your neighbor die? Didn't that other man have an accident? Didn't that woman's roof collapse on top of her? Didn't that other man drown? Didn't you see someone walking just the other day, almost in front of your door, who had a heart attack and passed away? In which language then could I have more clearly told you?"

Grandfather's Friend

An old friend of my grandfather invited me to dinner. Everyone I visited treated me royally, because of who my grandfather was—he was so well respected. I arrived at his house. The old man sat down, and so did I. He sat there for half an hour without speaking.

When the silence became too uncomfortable for me, I said, "Such nice weather." He didn't say a word. Finally, I couldn't take it anymore, and I said, "I'm hungry!" His face lit up when he heard that. He stood up and left, came back and spread a tablecloth on the table. He left again, and came back with a large loaf of homemade bread and two big glasses of water. He sat down and began to eat. I didn't know whether to start eating, or wait for the rest of the meal. I couldn't believe *that* was the dinner he invited me to!

Finally, I started to eat. I could hear the sound of every bite of bread I took, and of each sip of water. And I could *feel* the old man throughout the meal. Every time I looked up, he was right there, as if nothing else existed but me, him, and the activity of eating at that moment in time. At long last, I got up to go. As I was walking out the door, he finally spoke. "I love your grandfather as much as I love life."

From that day on, I receive a gift whenever I eat. What better food could he have given me?

A Fundamental Question

There was a school of philosophy in New York City. One question they ask you in that school is: "There's a man standing on a firm foundation, shaking. And there's a man standing firm on a shaky foundation. Which one is better off?"

Don't Eat Dates

A man brought his son to a wise man. "For God's sake, tell this son of mine not to eat dates! He's always under the tree eating dates and dates and dates! You're the only one he'll listen to. Tell him to stop!" The wise man thought for a moment, then said, "Come back tomorrow."

The next day, the man returned with his son. The wise man turned to the boy and said, "Don't eat so many dates. Every now and then is okay."

They left. And from that day on, the son ate dates only now and then. But the man was bothered by one thing. Why did the wise man send them all the way home, just to come back the next day. Why didn't he just tell his son that first day?

Finally, he set out for the wise man's house. He found him, and said, "Thank you for your help, but there's something on my mind. Why didn't you tell us the *first* day?" The wise man smiled and said, "Well, that day I ate dates."

32

Pay First

There's a saying: "First pay for the necessities, then indulge."

Not Now

A man came home one evening and found his wife sitting in the corner. In those days, you know, they didn't have electricity. Anyway, she was sewing, mending some clothes.

"Hi," said the man. "How are you?"

His wife didn't answer.

"Hello!" he said again.

"Yeah, yeah. Hi," she answered, without looking up.

"I want to talk to you," he said.

"No, no. Not now. Later," she said without missing a stitch.

He bent down and stuck his face in front of her.

"Husband, don't you know what this is?" his wife asked, exasperated.

"It's a candle," he said.

"What's happening to this candle?" she asked him.

"It's burning."

"You see!" she exclaimed. "That means this light is not going to last forever. While it exists, let me accomplish something."

34

Water to the Thirsty

Buddha said: "Water to the thirsty is precious. A mile to the tired is endless."

The Grateful Thief

Once there was a thief. He decided to rob the house of a rich man. He snuck into the bedroom and silently searched everywhere. Finally, he found the treasure box. Without a sound, he picked the lock and filled his sack with the rich man's gold and money. He crept towards the door.

The rich man, who had been asleep through all this, turned fitfully. His eyes opened and came to rest directly on the treasure box, whose lid was wide open. Realizing what had happened, he jumped out of bed and sprang at the thief, who was already closing the door behind him. He caught the thief's wrist in his iron grip.

The thief took a long, slow breath, and sighed deeply. "Thank you," he said.

The rich man was astonished. "What!" he said. "Why are you thanking me? And I heard it in your voice. You are sincere! How could you be grateful?"

"For years I've been a thief," he answered. "And I'm *very* good at it. I have only one weakness. But it makes me tremble. Not knowing what it's like to be caught. Now I know. You've made me free! Thank you!"

What Are You Thinking?

There's a place where they don't ask, "What are you thinking?" They say, "What is your mind chewing on?"

What Is Truth?

Someone asked a wise man, "What is Truth?"

The wise man said, "I'm going to give you one good answer: If you subtract everything you've added, what remains is Truth."

The Wise Man's Donkey

A man had a donkey who never did what he wanted him to. If he said "Walk," the donkey would stop. If he said "Stop," the donkey would break into a run. When the man tried to load him up with boxes, the donkey would suck in air and puff up his belly like crazy. As soon as the painstaking task of tying up all the supplies was completed, the donkey would let his air out so the ropes would slacken and all the crates would fall off and break. The man kicked him and beat him with a stick, but the donkey only got worse. Finally, he went to see a wise man whose donkey was always well-behaved.

"How come my donkey behaves like my worst enemy, and yours acts like an angel?" he asked.

"What's your relationship with him?" the wise man asked.

"What do you mean, 'relationship'? I'm the master, and he's just a donkey. A stupid donkey."

"Well," the wise man said, "it's a little different with my donkey. One day each week, I share my dinner with him, and then we go out together and have a good time."

Something About Myself

A student went to a Master and said, "I see something about myself that makes my blood boil!"

"Well," the Master told him, "you won't have blood forever."

They Asked the Seed

They came and asked the seed, "What are you doing here, all wrapped up in a hard shell?" "Well," said the seed, "with my shell, I feel very secure."

When the seed was in the soil, they asked, "What are you doing here?" "I am very comfortable," said the seed, "because my grandfather says that darkness is the beginning of the light."

When the seed started to grow in the soil, they asked, "How are you?" "Good," he answered, "because the soil is hard and growth is difficult. This will make me strong, so that when I am in the sunshine, I will not wither."

When the seed sprouted above the ground and grew very quickly, they asked, "Why are you growing so fast?" "Because I have been waiting a long time."

When it became a tree, they asked, "What are you doing?" "I am growing branches and leaves to pay back my mother, by giving her some shade."

When it was full of leaves, they asked, "What are you doing?" "I am making flowers to improve the atmosphere."

When it was full of flowers, they asked, "What is it you are doing?" "I am making fruit to help others."

When it was a seed again, they asked, "What are you doing?" Seed said, "Isn't it obvious?"

How Old Is Your Body?

There was once a place where, when it was someone's birthday, people never asked, "How old are you?" They asked, "How old is your body?" They never asked, "How are you?" They'd say, "How is your body?" Because who is that *you,* anyway? And they never said, "So and so died." They said, "He left this planet."

The Great Gambler

There was a man who considered himself a great gambler. One day, he went to see the most famous gambler in the world.

They sat down and began to play. The man who considered himself a great gambler bet ten dollars. He lost it. He bet one hundred dollars. He lost that. He bet a thousand. And lost. So he bet a million (he was a wealthy man), but he lost it. Finally, he lost all his money. But he continued to gamble, hoping he could win it back. He bet his house, but he lost. He bet his watch, and lost it. So he bet his shirt. And lost. He bet his pants. He lost.

Finally, he stood up next to the table, in only his underpants. "Well," he said, "I am defeated."

The famous gambler looked at him and said, "You are not a real gambler."

"What do you mean? I staked everything I had, even my house, even my clothes!"

"No," said the legendary gambler. "You're still wearing your underpants."

Your Skin Has to Shine

There's a saying: "Your skin has to shine more than your clothes."

At the Party

A man was invited to a very important party. He worked late in his fields that day, and went straight to the party in his work clothes. He was greeted coolly, and was seated by himself near the door. The servants didn't even bring him any food. He sat there for a while, and then got up and left.

He ran home, threw off his work clothes, and put on his best robe. It was beautifully woven with many gold and silver threads, and precious stones were sewn around the collar. The back was exquisitely embroidered. He ran back to the party.

This time, when he walked in, everyone stood up in admiration. The servants ushered him to a chair at the host's table. They immediately brought plates and bowls, and gave him a large serving of a rich, aromatic soup. The man lifted his right arm, and put his sleeve in the soup. "There," he said. "Good. Eat." Then he lifted his left arm, and dunked his other sleeve in the soup. "Eat, yes, good, eat," he said. Then he leaned forward and dipped the front of his robe in the soup. "Please. Eat, eat. Yes, good…"

"What are you doing, for God's sake?" his horrified host asked.

The man pointed to the robe, and said, "Well, you invited *him*."

At a Bus Stop

Two guys were standing at a bus stop in New York City, waiting for the bus. One of them reached down to the sidewalk, brought his hand up to his mouth, and started making loud chewing sounds. He bent down again, made a scooping motion with both hands and brought them to his mouth. "Chacchhh, chacchhh."

"Whadaya doin'?" the other man asked.

"I'm eating. Khchhh, khcch-ch-ch, khchh, ch-ch-ch." He continued to chomp.

"Whadaya eatin'?"

"Rocks. Kch-ch-ch, kh-ch-ch-ch, kh-ch-ch-ch."

"What kinda rocks?"

"Imaginary rocks. Kch-ch-ch-ch."

"Ya know," the other man told him seriously, "if you're gonna eat imaginary food, ya might as well eat imaginary caviar."

God and the Devil

A student once asked, "What's the difference between God and the devil?"

The Master replied, "God knows he has a devil in himself. The devil hasn't experienced God within himself yet."

My Desire

A Master once said, "If your desire to see is strong enough, it will lead you to see everything."

Eat Dates or Pray

It was said that Moses was walking in the desert. He came upon a man sitting next to a bowl of dates. The man was praying and eating the dates. "Either pray or eat dates!" Moses told him, and walked on.

Several days later, the same man passed by, and saw Moses sitting and praying and eating dates. He hid himself behind a rock and watched to be sure that it really was Moses sitting there, eating a date and praying.

When he was sure, he went up to Moses and said, "You can't do that!" Moses kept doing it. "You can't do that!" he shouted. "Either pray or eat dates!" Moses kept chewing.

After a while, the man said, "Would you tell me something? When you told *me* not to do that, I stopped right away. Now I told you not to. How come you do what you told me not to do?" Moses smiled. He took another bite and said, "This is how I pray."

Seven Levels of Heaven

A wise old man once said to his son:

The entire sky

The seven levels of Heaven

Are working ceaselessly

Are striving constantly

Are moving endlessly

Just to create a possibility

For you

To gain a grain of wisdom.

Is it fair to stay in bed?

Don't Forget Death

The people in one town, instead of saying, "Hello, how are you?" would say, "Brother, don't forget your death."

His Whole Life

They asked a wise man, "Why is it, and how is it, that God managed not to sleep?"

The wise man said, "Because he realized his whole life is but one moment."

The Canary

A man had a canary in a cage. Day and night, the canary sang the most beautiful songs. One day, the man came home, and the first thing he heard was the lovely song of his canary. He went and stood by the cage. "God," he thought to himself, "I can't understand it. I always feel so sorry for this poor bird, whose whole life is spent in a cage. But here he is, singing with such joy."

He bent down to the canary and said, "Could you answer a question? How could you be so happy in this cage?" The bird stopped singing. He looked at the man and said, "Be reasonable! I'm in this cage, that's true. But since I know I'm a bird, it's good to sing."

"Did You Hear Me?"

They have a very beautiful expression in one little town. When two people are talking, one might say, "Did you hear me?" meaning, "Did we communicate? Is there an understanding between us?" The other one answers, "I heard you, but I don't know with whose ear!"

The Skeptical Man

A very skeptical man was walking down the street one day, when he saw a gold coin lying in the road. He went and picked it up, looked at it and thought, "It certainly looks like gold." But he wasn't one hundred percent sure. He tried biting it, he rubbed it, he examined it in every way. Everything indicated it really was gold. But still he doubted his luck. "If it really *is* gold, why hasn't someone taken it already?"

Finally, he had an idea. "Let's see what someone else thinks." So he put the coin back in the road, and he went and hid around the corner to watch what would happen. Pretty soon, another man came along and saw the coin. He picked it up, then raised his hands up to the sky and shouted, "Thank God!" And he put it in his pocket and walked away.

The Soldier with the Wooden Sword

There was once a soldier, the greatest soldier of his time. Everyone spoke about his great bravery and his legendary sword. As a student, he was known for his clarity and perseverance.

One day, a group of soldiers came across him sitting on a stone wall. His famous sword hung from his belt, and a long wooden stick rested on his lap. He was totally absorbed in whittling the stick, slowly fashioning it into a sword. The soldiers, struck by his calmness and the way he focused all his attention on that single task, stood there watching him. But he never looked up. It seemed as if he, the stick, and the activity of whittling were one inseparable thing. Finally, one of them asked, "Why is it the devil is never bothering you?"

He answered him with his hand, slowly scraping his knife down the wooden stick, and then drawing it back toward himself again. "Here's the answer," he said, picking up the stick. "This is how I keep the devil away."

"With *that* sword?" he asked. "You've got the mightiest sword in the world hanging at your waist. Why do you need a wooden sword to hold off the devil?"

"No, no," he answered. "It's not the sword, it's the *making* of the sword that keeps him away."

Poetry About God

To write poetry about God is one thing. To shake hands with God is another story.

Truth

Truth has a ring to it. You hear it—you wake up.

Are You Praying?

A man came upon a group of people praying. He went up to one of them and said, "Are you praying?" He raised his head up, said, "Yes," and lowered his head again. The man went up to another guy and asked, "Are you praying?" He made a hand motion to indicate "yes." The man went to another guy. "Are you praying?" He nodded his head. He went to another man, and asked. Without raising his head, the man whispered, "Yes."

Finally, he went up to a man and said, "Are you praying?" No answer. **"Are you praying?"** No answer. **"ARE YOU PRAYING?"** No answer. "Thank you very much," the man said. "You *are* praying!"

The Ladder

An old man was carrying a ladder. He got to his house, and leaned the ladder against the wall. He stepped up onto the first rung, then stepped off. "I *hate* this ladder," he said. He stepped up again, but stepped right off again. He took a step or two back, and said, "I *hate* this ladder!" He kept stepping on and off, and complaining. A neighbor, who saw the whole thing, finally asked him, "Why do you hate the ladder?"

"Because I love *that* ladder." He pointed at nothing in particular.

"Which one?"

"That one." He pointed again. But there was nothing, just one ladder leaning against the house.

"Which one?"

"THAT ONE!" he yelled, and pointed.

"But I don't see another ladder," the neighbor said.

"It's an imaginary ladder," he explained.

"Why do you like it so much better than this one?"

"Because it's easy to climb!"

The Thirsty Bird

In the hottest part of the country, two brothers were working in their field. A bird that was circling overhead alighted on a bush. One of the brothers walked up to the bird, poured some water from his goatskin into his palm, and held his hand out to the bird. The bird drank, and the man poured more water for her.

The other brother came over to watch. "Why are you doing that?" he asked, slightly annoyed. You see, they barely had enough water to feed their crops, and it seldom rained.

"I don't know," his brother answered. "But it feels like the right thing." And he continued pouring water for the thirsty bird.

The next year, there was a terrible drought. No rain fell, and there was no water to be had. The entire country was parched and dry. But the garden of the two brothers was still beautiful. It was full of lush, green plants in full bloom. No one understood it. Finally, their next-door neighbor, consumed by curiosity, broke down and came to them. "How do you do this?" he asked. "And in the midst of this drought!"

"Come see our secret," the brother said.

He led his neighbor to a corner of the garden. The air was thick with hundreds of birds. They circled, alighted briefly on the ground and flew off. Immediately, another flock of birds came. As they landed, they each opened their beaks, depositing a few drops of water next to one of the plants. Then they flew off again, traveling a great distance to fetch a few drops more for the garden of their friend.

To See Everything

There's a saying: "If you want to see everything as it really is, look with the eyes of God."

The Last Day of the Devil

Well, a day came, the last day of the devil. The archangels came and got him, and then they opened his file. "Ooh, ooh, ooh, ooh, ooh! What a record. *Straight* to hell!" They grabbed him and took him to the edge of the abyss, to throw him down to hell. The devil kicked and struggled wildly.

"What!" they said. "With a record like that you still have the nerve to resist?"

"I resist!" screamed the devil, still kicking.

"Why?" the archangels asked. "Why do you resist?"

"You ask the Lord," the devil said. "He knows how much good I've done. I deserve a little break." The archangels looked at each other. "No way!" they said with one voice.

They grabbed his hands and feet, and swung him over the abyss—one, two, three, and… Well, the devil cried and screamed so loud, they put him down again. "Maybe, who knows?" they said. They went to God.

"What should we do with him?" they asked.

"Did you read his file?"

"Yes, Lord."

"How is it?"

"*Direct* to hell."

"Throw him into hell," God said.

They took the devil back to the abyss. One, two, three… But again he cried and screamed so loud, they stopped. "One more time," he screamed. "Call God one more time, and tell him to give me just a *tiny* bit of help."

They asked God again. This time he said, "All right. As I remember, he once did something good. Maybe we should give him a little help. Let's give him a small hint. When you throw him into the abyss, ask him this question: 'Are you made of fire or soil?' If he says 'soil,' he'll be saved. If he says, 'fire,' he will burn."

So they brought the devil to the edge, and one, two, THREE, they cast him into the abyss. "Are you made of fire or soil?" they shouted after him.

Down went the devil, falling through space, tumbling and turning, as he grappled with God's question. Just as he neared the bottom of the pit, and was about to fall into the river that flowed in through the gates of hell, he shouted "SOIL!"

Then he landed softly on his feet on the bank of the river.

And that's why the devil is still around.

A Wrestling Match

A man once led his grandson to a dark room and said, "I want you to wrestle with this guy. When you've knocked him to the ground, call me. I'll be waiting outside." Then he shut the door.

It was pitch black inside, and the boy couldn't see anyone. So he waited. Nothing happened. After a while, he started to feel stupid. "Maybe he was serious," the boy thought. "Maybe there's someone here and I don't know it."

He started to jump around, and threw punches everywhere. He jabbed, feinted, and punched until he was totally exhausted. Suddenly, the door opened, and his grandfather took him outside. "That's what happens when you have an imaginary enemy," he said.

The New Porsche

There was a man who was very successful in business. He was always telling me, "You have to see the possibilities. That's the key to success."

He went and bought a brand new Porsche—the most deluxe convertible model. Less than a week later, he drove to a restaurant in Los Angeles to meet some people. After the meeting, they said good night, and he went to the parking lot.

He was just getting into the car, when a man appeared out of nowhere, put a gun to his temple, and said, "Put the key in the ignition, and step aside." He did as he was told. The thief got behind the wheel, started the car, and drove away. The man was in shock for three days.

"What for?" I said to him. "That was beautiful."

"What do you mean, 'beautiful'?" he asked.

"You saw the possibilities."

Children

Two good friends were talking about their children. "One thing is obvious," one of them said to the other. "We *have* to find a way so they don't become like us!"

King Solomon's Temple

When King Solomon decided to build the temple, he collected materials from every corner of the Earth. He brought the greatest architects and engineers to build it. Thousands of workers spent many years on it, and when it was finished, it was the largest and the most magnificent structure on Earth. Then Solomon invited all the people to the temple, and he himself came to give the first sermon.

After he spoke, he saw something. In one corner of the temple, a tiny weed was growing between two large stones.

King Solomon knew the languages of all the animals and all the plants. So he went to the weed and said, "Hello, stranger. I've never seen you before. What is your name?" And the weed answered him, "My name is Kharouk."

Solomon asked him, "What is your function on this planet?" And Kharouk answered him, "My job is to grow wherever there stands a building that should not be. My root shakes the foundation in such a way that the building falls."

Without another word, King Solomon ran to the podium and yelled for everyone to get out immediately. The crowd streamed out of the temple, and a moment later, the majestic structure collapsed.

That night, the King walked among the ruins of the once splendid temple. Suddenly, he saw one of Kharouk's small green leaves peeking out from underneath an enormous marble column. "Tell me, my tiny friend, why was the temple destroyed?"

"You see," said Kharouk, "the form was stronger than the content, so destruction was inevitable."

Sayings

When the heart is touched,
the mind becomes quiet.

First fill up your jug by collecting dewdrops.
Then it will rain.

Lying next to a running river, under the shade
of a big tree, the summer sun is pleasant.

Your body is your friend when you know it.
Your feeling is your friend when you experience it.
Your mind is your friend when you use it.

As a river flows, it fills up each depression it comes to, then flows on. Live your life like a river; penetrate the depth of each moment.

There is knowing even when you don't know.

A flower blooms in your garden because its root was nurtured.

Friends support your weaknesses. Enemies show your need for strength.

Death is a point in life.
Life is a point in eternity.
Eternity is a point in now.
Now is a point in this moment.

Look at the bright side of life
without turning from the dark side.

The sound is there before you hear it.
Love is there before you feel it.
Peace is there before you think it.
Existence is there even if you aren't.

*By striving to fulfill your financial needs honestly,
you may learn your real need.*

*Give when you don't have.
Receive when you don't want.
Be when you are not.*

Ask your mind, but listen to your heart.

Looking for the Star of Wisdom

There was an old man. Every single night, he would walk outside, raise his head up, and close his eyes. One day, his grandson asked him, "Grandfather, what is it you are doing every night?"

"I'm looking for the Star of Wisdom," he said.

"But you always close your eyes! When I want to see the stars, I keep my eyes wide open."

Chance Meetings

A man was standing in the street somewhere near Times Square waving his arms all around. "What are you doing?" I asked him.

"I'm balancing the energy of the planets, and the Milky Way, and the stars. You see, a couple of stars were in a fight, but now I've patched things up."

A few blocks away, another man bent down and touched the ground with the tip of his index finger, and then touched his fingertip to his palm. When I walked over to him, he held out his hand and asked, "What do you see?" The way he asked, and the way he was looking at his palm, I knew he wanted me to say something. I was afraid to say I only saw a little dust or something.

"What is it?" the man asked.
"I…I really don't see anything."
"Nothing?" he asked, incredulously.
"No."
"Billions and billions of stars!" he shouted. "The whole UNIVERSE!"

Not far away, there was a man who was sweeping the sidewalk in front of a big office building. I stopped to watch him. There was something so pleasing about the way he swept. He caught every scrap of dirt, too.

"Why so careful?" I asked him.

"I like it to be really clean," he said. "Sometimes God comes here, you know, and dances on this spot."

How Can I Benefit?

A Master was sitting down to drink tea when he heard a knock at the door. In walked a student, with bent shoulders, who (without taking his eyes off the ground) asked, "Master, how could I benefit from my sadness?" The Master told him, "Go look in the mirror. Without changing what you see, laugh at what you see." The student nodded his head, and left.

The Master returned to his teapot and poured himself a cup of tea, but again there was a knock at the door. In came another student, smiling as though he could hardly contain himself. "Master," he asked, "how do I benefit by my happiness?" The Master answered, "Go look in the mirror. Without changing what you see, cry for what you see." The student thanked him, and left.

Bread and Water

This is a children's story. It happened that a poor man was going to have an important guest to his house for dinner. He usually ate very simply, grinding his own flour, making bread, and fetching water from the nearby stream for tea. But he thought maybe he should get something better to serve his special guest.

He went to town thinking, "I'll get some yogurt for my guest." He went to the man who sold yogurt and asked, "Do you have special yogurt?"

"Oh, yes," said the yogurt man. "My yogurt is as rich as butter." The simple man said, "Thank you very much," and left, thinking that if the yogurt man was comparing his yogurt to butter, butter must be more special than yogurt.

So he went to the woman who sold butter and asked, "Do you have butter that is very special?" The butter seller told him, "Oh, yes, my friend, my butter is so wonderful, it's as smooth as olive oil." When the man heard that, he said, "Thank you very much," and left in search of the man who sold olive oil.

When he found the olive oil seller, he asked him, "Do you have olive oil that's very special?" "That I do," replied the olive oil man. "My olive oil is as pure as good spring water." When the simple man heard that, he said, "Thank you very much," and went home to prepare for his guest, very pleased to already have the most special things.

The Lonely Doctor

Did you hear about the doctor who went to set up a new practice?

He opened an office, and stayed there constantly, but no patients came. One month passed. No patients. Two months passed. No one. Three months. Six months. A year went by. Finally, he went to his next-door neighbor and said, "What am I doing wrong?"

His neighbor looked puzzled. "Why do you ask?"

"For one whole year I've had my clinic here, and no one has come!"

"Well, your clinic is for sick people, that's why no one comes."

"What kind of town is this?" the doctor asked.

"This is the town of Wisdom," his neighbor said. "People eat when they're hungry, and they eat only as much as they need."

Gandhi

A man took a class in Indian history. One day, his teacher told him that whenever Gandhi wanted to motivate people towards goodness, he stopped eating. The man thought about it, and decided to try the same thing. So he fasted, but the world didn't change for the better. As far as he could see, nothing happened at all.

Later, he told his teacher about it. The teacher said, "First become Gandhi, then your fast will have an effect."

"I Can't!"

There was once a little boy who felt so discouraged. He went to his grandfather and said, "I can't."

His grandfather looked at him with eyes full of kindness, and said, "That's a good time to let God help."

Moving the Tree

One spring, after an especially snowy winter, the stream near one village became swollen with water and difficult to cross. The townspeople decided to build a bridge by laying a big tree across the stream.

Well, there was one giant old tree that had died that winter. They cut it down, and then about thirty people came to carry it to the stream. They lifted it up, and then fifteen of them started to walk, supporting the tree on one shoulder. Just then, a wise man passed by. When he saw them, he shouted, "You people don't know what it means to work together. Why are only half of you working?"

"But there's only room for fifteen to carry the tree!" they protested.

"If only fifteen can carry it on their shoulders, the rest of you should put your hands under the tree to help support it. If there's not enough room to do that, then you should place a hand on the back of someone who is carrying the tree. And if there's not enough room to touch them, you should *look* at them, and give them your attention. *That's* what it means to work together!"

On Love

Either you love, or you lie.

Love for life begins when you become capable of loving another human being. But this love must be unconditional. You don't love *him,* you don't love *her.* Your love exists, then other people exist in that love. Then *everything* exists in that love. If you love, nothing is excluded. Love which is for this, and not for that, has opposition. Love which has opposition is not love, because its source isn't Truth. Truth has no opposition. It embraces its opposition, and so transforms it within itself.

A Grain of Truth

A great poet once said, "I took a thousand wrong turns in my journey for Truth. But when I arrived, I found all those turns had been necessary."

The Cake

There's a custom in some parts of the world. When someone dies, their family prepares a large tray of sweets. And for forty days, they offer some to everyone who passes by the deceased's house. As people pass, they take a sweet from the tray, and they say something nice, like "May God bless the soul of the man who left this planet."

There was a guy who always made a point of knowing who had died, because that information was a good source of food. One day, when he was especially craving something sweet, he walked home, making sure to pass by the house of the wealthy man who had died just the day before. As he walked, he thought about the delicious treats he might get, and composed a flowery speech about the dead man.

When he got to the man's house, a woman held out a huge tray with one tiny piece of cake on it. The man looked at the little piece of cake, and wondered if there was another tray about to be brought out. "How much cake is there?" he asked hopefully, recalling his speech.

"How much cake is there?" the woman repeated. "Just a thank you's worth."

The Mustache

There was once a man who had a very famous tea shop that served the best coffee and pastries. He was famous not only for his tea shop, but also because he had a gigantic mustache that ran from his nose to his shoulders. Literally. And it was carefully curled at the ends. Anyone who saw him from a distance, even from the back, could tell it was him.

A friend of his walked into his tea shop, and saw him gripping a customer by the shoulders, and shaking him as hard as he could.

"I'm going to kill this monster!" he shouted.

"Why? What happened?" his friend asked.

Slowly he let go of the customer. He took a deep breath, and let out a long sigh. "Everything was fine. Then two weeks ago, he came in here, and asked me if I sleep with my mustache under the covers or on top of the covers. That damn question! I'd never thought of it! So I tried tucking it under the blanket, but it didn't feel right. I tried spreading it on top of the blanket, but that didn't feel right either. Why did he have to ask me that? I haven't slept for two weeks!"

Wisdom

A man who was generally regarded as both wise and simple was riding down the street on his donkey, when a friend stopped him, and asked, "Tell me, where did you get your wisdom?" The man looked at him and asked, "What day is today?"

"Thursday," his friend said.

"I can't answer your question today. Only on Friday." He continued on his way. The next day, he was passing by the same street. When his friend saw him, he ran after him and said, "Today is Friday. Answer my question!"

The man climbed down off his donkey. The donkey was loaded with crates. In one crate were twenty Bibles. Another contained twenty books of Eastern religious wisdom. A third crate was filled with books of religious poetry. The man was on his way to deliver them to a seller of holy books. He stood in front of his donkey, and said to him, "So now there's a question for us, my friend. The question is, 'Where did we get our wisdom?'"

The donkey just stood there. The man turned to his friend, and gave him a puzzled look. Again he put his face close to his donkey's, and asked, "Where did we get our wisdom?" The donkey stood there and swished his tail at a fly. The man turned to his friend and said, "Look at that. *He* is carrying a thousand books of wisdom, and won't say a word. Why should *I* say anything?"

King Solomon and the Fox

When Fox heard that King Solomon was going to choose an animal to be in charge of all the animals, he decided it had to be him. He ran to the street of the potters, and snuck into the master potter's studio. There he hid until nightfall. When everyone left, he uncovered all the glaze pots, and dipped his tail into each one until he had painted himself from head to foot with beautiful colors. Then he ran out of the studio and hid by the palace road, waiting for King Solomon's entourage to pass.

When the King's guards approached, he bolted between their legs and ran straight up to the King.

"I am a peacock," he began, out of breath, "and the most beautiful of God's creatures. Choose me to govern the other animals!"

As soon as Fox finished speaking, it began to rain hard. In seconds, he turned into a bedraggled mess. The paints ran down his face and body, stung his eyes, and dripped all over the ground. He stood there with his head lowered, ashamed to look up.

Solomon looked at him and smiled. "You are not a peacock as you claim, my friend, but a fox. A very sorry fox. But your experience may give you something that other animals don't have. So I hereby appoint you steward of all the animals!"

"Oh-Ho-Ho"

There was once a Buddhist monk. Whenever things became difficult, he'd say, "Oh-ho-ho," in a slow, deep voice that sounded like a recording of a bass singer being played at slow speed.

Once someone asked him, "Are you complaining or chanting?" He said, "What's the use of complaining if there's no chanting in it? What's the value of chanting if there's no complaining in it?"

The Frustrated Thief

One night a thief slipped in through a wise man's window. He crept all through the house, searching every room for valuables, but found nothing worth taking. The whole family was sleeping soundly, oblivious to the intruder. Finally, after searching the man's bedroom, the thief, tense and exasperated, bent down and grabbed him by the shoulders and shook him violently.

"Why is it you look so rich, but when I get here, you're so poor?" he shouted.

The wise man looked at him without expression. "How many houses have you robbed?" he asked.

"Many, many," the thief answered.

"Has this ever happened to you before?" he asked.

"Never," he said.

"You should be grateful," he told him. "My life is so simple, it could even give a hardened thief like you a new experience. What's more precious than that?"

Accepting the Devil

They asked the prophet Moses, "Why is God stronger than the devil?"

Moses smiled, and said, "Because God accepts the devil. His world is so complete, it even has room for the devil to fit in. But the devil doesn't have the ability to accept God. His world is so small, God does not fit in."

Shopping

One day a man went shopping in the bazaar. First he stopped and bought some wool for a new suit. He loaded it onto his horse, and went to the cobbler's to buy a pair of slippers for his wife. As soon as he went inside, some thieves stole the woolen fabric off his horse. The man came out, packed the slippers into the saddlebag, and continued to the spice sellers. The thieves followed him, and as soon as he went to buy saffron, they stole the slippers out of the saddlebag. While he was buying onions, they stole the saffron. This went on for quite a while.

Finally, a friend of his saw what was going on, and ran up to inform him. "Hey! Thieves are stealing each thing you buy the minute you put it on your horse!"

"I know," the man told him. "But today I'm in the mood to buy, and I'm having the time of my life!"

The Magic Tree

In a small village was a very tall tree. Even kids who loved to climb had a hard time climbing it. Once, one boy got really sick. One of the villagers told him, "If you wanna get cured, climb that tree!" And he pointed to the giant tree.

Well, the boy dragged himself out of bed, and climbed it. When he got back down, he was cured! For years he believed that tree was magic. Then he learned it wasn't the tree. He was so scared when he climbed it, he was sweating like crazy. The sweating cured him.

Do You Think I'm Great?

There was once a man who was a fluent philosopher, a gifted writer, an exceptional poet, and a profound mystic. A group of admirers came to visit him. They fawned over him, and praised all his works. He turned to them suddenly and asked, "Do you think I'm great?"

"Of course," they all said.

"Now come here," he told his guests. He led them to his yard, where there was a tall date tree. He picked up a date pit from the ground, held it up next to the tree, and said, "Do you still think I'm great?"

If Your Enemy Is Wise

If your enemy is wise, you may lose, but with much profit.

God Is Generous

There was a man whose roof leaked for years. Finally, he decided to have it fixed. He hired workmen who tore the old roof completely off, planning to replace it the next day with a new one. The night before they planned to do the work, the head carpenter got sick, and so the roofers didn't come that day.

The man decided to go to the market. When he got there, he couldn't remember what he was supposed to buy, so he left empty-handed. On his way home, the temperature dropped suddenly. The wind stopped for a moment, and it began to snow. Then he remembered his nonexistent roof. "God is generous!" he said out loud, and quickened his pace.

Nearing his house, he gave a start as he remembered that all his relatives were coming to visit that day. "God is generous!" he said out loud, and hurried on.

As he reached his doorstep, he ran into the mailman, who handed him an official-looking envelope. He tore it open, and found a summons to appear in court that day for unpaid debts. "God is generous!" he said to the mailman.

He opened the door and found his house so full with people he had to suck in his breath just to squeeze in. He called to his wife, suddenly remembering that she was expecting. Just then, a cheer arose, as the midwives came out of the bedroom carrying triplets.

"God is generous," the man said. "But I didn't know he was *that* generous!"

The Mountain Climber

One day, a mountain climber found a man sitting at the foot of a tall mountain, crying and praying. He ignored the man, and started up the mountain. The next day, he went to climb the mountain again, and there was the man sitting in the same spot, crying and praying. "Well," he said to himself, "none of my business, really." So he hiked on.

The day after that, he set out to climb the mountain a third time. This time, when he spotted the man, he couldn't resist. "What's the matter? Why are you crying?" he asked.

"Because I didn't learn to pray sincerely," the man told him.

The climber continued on his way, but the man stuck in his mind. Although he had enough of that mountain, he went back the next day to see if the man was still crying there. Sure enough, he was there, still weeping and praying.

"Forgive me, but may I ask what is it you are praying for?"

"I'm praying to be on the peak of this tall mountain," he said.

"Every day I'm on the peak of this mountain. And I never prayed, I just climbed."

A Friend from the Country

There was a man who came from the countryside. He was eighty-seven years old. He ate three figs a day, and a little hot milk in the evening. Nothing else. And he had tremendous energy and a very sharp, perceptive mind.

One day, he went to visit a friend in the big city. They walked all day, and sat up all night discussing what they saw, and how to make sense of life on this planet. Actually, his city friend sat—*he* stood on his head the whole time.

One day, they went to visit a very wealthy man. He lived in a spectacular mansion on the Hudson River near New York City. First he showed them around, pointing out his antique French furniture with great pride. Then he ushered them into the salon for tea.

"Here is my most prized piece," he said, indicating a large couch. It was elegantly carved, and upholstered with the most delicately embroidered silk.

The old man immediately sat down on it. He bounced around a little, testing its resilience, and then tucked his legs up into the lotus position. The host stood there, stunned by this shocking behavior. Just then, a servant wheeled in a cart and served tea. The old man sat there on the couch, holding the saucer and sipping his tea with relish. The host finally sat down, but his face was ashen. He never took his eyes off the old man's hands. He was afraid that at any moment this crazy old man would spill tea on his priceless couch.

Finally, he pulled himself together a little. "How do you like my house?" he asked in a strained voice. The old man bounced a few times on the couch. He took another sip of tea, smiled, and answered, "So comfortable for me. So miserable for you."

The Lucky Merchant

Once there was a merchant. After years of "business as usual," his luck took a sudden turn. Everything he purchased, he bought for pennies. Everything he sold, he sold dear. And the more he succeeded, the more successful he became. Finally, he decided to come to terms with his sudden prosperity. First, he took a whole year off and traveled around the world.

"A man of my stature should be well traveled," he thought to himself. When he returned, his business was flourishing and his riches had multiplied, thanks to his most competent supervisor. And everyone now called him "sir." This pleased him. "A man like me should have fine clothes," he said to himself. So he sent for the tailor and had an exquisite wardrobe made for his whole family, dressing them in the costliest silks. Then he decided that his house no longer suited him.

"A man of my rank and position needs a house that reflects his great honor," he decided. So he opened his coffers, and called the best builders in his town and all their apprentices. He brought the best artisans, and entire workshops emptied out to work on his new house. "I want the biggest house in town," he proclaimed. And so it was. He was beside himself with pride.

Now, in that part of the world, all the houses are built with flat roofs. And all the roofs are thatched with straw and mud. They hold up well in almost all types of weather. They're cool in summer, and warm in winter. They dry quickly after a rainstorm. But if it snows, the moisture soaks into the straw, and the roofs crack and break. Fortunately, it seldom snows, and when it does, each man climbs onto his roof immediately to sweep the snow off, before the moisture does any damage.

Well, one night that winter, it snowed there as it never had before. Even the nearby desert turned white.

When the merchant awoke, he took one look at the snow, and his heart almost stopped. He climbed onto his roof with a broom and started sweeping furiously. Soon he realized he was getting nowhere. So he ran to the town, and had all the poor men rush to his house with shovels and brooms. He immediately set them to work clearing the snow from his roof.

They worked feverishly, but his house was so enormous, they could clear only a small part of the roof. The merchant ran back to town, and grabbed everyone he could find to come sweep his roof. They swept and swept, but the roof was too big. Again, he raced to town. He ran from house to house, begging, threatening, and bribing, until everyone in town was standing in line with a shovel or broom. He returned to his mansion with an army of workers.

They spread out over the roof and began digging as though possessed, while the man ran from here to there yelling, "Faster, faster." Soon it became apparent that even the entire town couldn't clear the roof. It was just too big. Then it started to snow again.

The merchant wandered about in a daze, watching the townspeople dig frantically. But the snow covered even the areas they had already cleared. He realized that his house was ruined, and all was lost.

He entered his house and walked slowly through each room, looking at every detail. Last, he entered the smallest room, which served as a storage closet for valuables. He found an oil lamp, lit it, placed it on the floor, and turned slowly in a circle, looking at all his possessions. Then, with the sounds of the commotion on the roof filtering softly into the room, he knelt down and prayed for the first time since he had become wealthy.

"I wish my relationship to God to always be bigger than my roof," he said. And when he looked up, he saw the first rays of sunlight shining in through the window.

A Case of Gold

A man was sitting on a rock, overlooking the ocean. Next to him was a case filled with gold coins. The man picked up a coin, studied it, and then threw it into the ocean. He picked out another coin, turned it over in his hand, and flung it into the sea.

A wandering monk was passing by, and stopped to look at this unusual performance. After seeing a good amount of gold disappear into the sea, he approached the man and said, "What is this?"

"A case of gold," the man answered.

"But what are you doing?" he asked.

"I'm throwing it into the ocean."

"Why do you want to do that?"

"I'm practicing non-attachment," he replied, calmly.

"Then why don't you just dump them all in at once?" asked the monk.

"Oh, no," he said. "This attachment I have, it needs to be struggled with a hundred thousand times."

Apple Pie

Remember the story of the two men who loved God? They were sitting in a restaurant, and the waiter, sensing something special about them, brought them each a big piece of apple pie. "This is on the house!" he said.

One of the men ate his pie with gusto. The other didn't touch his. When they walked out, he turned to his friend and said, "Boy, I don't know how you did that! The love of God was so present in me, I just had no desire for apple pie."

"For me, it was a little different," his friend answered. "The love of God was present, and the love of apple pie was present. So I shared my pie with God."

Intelligence

Someone asked a wise man, "Why is it you always talk like that? I've never heard you speak intelligently."

"You're right," he said. "Life is so precious, there's no time for intelligence."

Free Will

One night, a couple of friends were discussing the concept of free will. An old man, who was visiting one of them, interrupted. "Would you allow me to do something?"

"Please do," his friend told him.

He asked if anyone had some needles. Someone brought in a bunch of needles, and the old man placed them on the table. Then he asked someone to bring him a magnet from the kitchen. The old man held the magnet under the table, moved it around, and shouted excitedly, "Oh! The needles are moving! The needles are moving!"

Everyone was staring at the table. He looked at them and said, "That's what the needles think!"

The Beggar

There once was a beggar. Every morning he walked from the outskirts of town, past the university, and all the way to the center of the city to occupy his customary spot. There he would sit all day long, shaking his tin cup, and calling out blessings on the passersby who dropped something in it for him. At night, he counted up his pennies, bought some food at the corner grocery, and walked home.

Day after day, year after year, he followed the identical route, and the identical routine. A group of philosophy students saw the beggar pass by each day and became interested in him. "Everything in life changes," one philosophized. "And yet life goes on for this beggar in exactly the same way day after day."

"Man is a product of his environment," theorized another. "If this beggar had had different circumstances, he might not be a beggar at all."

And so they spoke, until one day, they decided to put their ideas to the test. They each chipped in one gold piece, and filled up a small chest with them. Early in the morning, they posted sentries along the beggar's route, and when he approached the bridge, they gave a signal. One of the students opened the chest of gold and placed it on the bridge exactly where the beggar was bound to see it. Then they all concealed themselves.

The beggar walked across the bridge, exactly as he did every day. He passed right by the chest of gold without missing a step, and continued on his way. The students recovered the chest, and followed him as far as the university. There they broke into a stormy debate, trying to prove and disprove each other's contentions based on the beggar's behavior that morning. Still unable to come to any agreement, they decided to ask the beggar what happened. They ran to his spot, where they found him rattling his cup as usual.

"Good morning, my dear man," one of the students began. "I have seen you walking here many times, as I take the same route myself, and have often thought to make your acquaintance. Tell me, didn't you notice something unusual this morning?"

"Why, yes. As a matter of fact, this very morning, I had the strangest thoughts," the beggar replied. "I thought of how we seem to follow the same patterns, passing our lifetimes without altering even the smallest detail. Then, as I got to the bridge, I wondered, 'What would it be like if I were blind?' So I decided to cross the bridge with my eyes closed."

Watching the Campfire

A group of travelers was passing through the mountains. Because there were many dangers and the land was unfamiliar, they kept a lookout each night. Their journey proceeded without incident, but when it was Jack's turn to watch, the travelers were nervous. Jack was a daydreamer and napper, who could hardly keep his eyes open even during the day. The other travelers didn't trust his ability to guard them during the night. They feared that if he slept, they might be attacked by wild animals or bandits. But they were exhausted from their journey, so they settled in for an uneasy night's sleep, leaving Jack to watch the campfire.

In the morning, the first thing they heard was the crackling of the campfire. They looked up, and there sat Jack, staring wide-eyed at the campfire. "Jack, you're a hero!" they called out to him. Jack turned to them, and in a strong voice said, "Don't call me a hero. Be grateful to all those mosquitoes!"

Wave Told Mountain

Wave once told Mountain, "Life is too short to spend it all in silence." And Mountain said, "By rushing it, you make it even shorter."

Wishful Thinking

A man had a streak of good luck. Whatever he wished for seemed to come true. He wished for rice pudding, and when he got home, his wife was just setting it on the table. He wished he could stop making furniture, and when he got to work, he found that he had been made a foreman.

He decided to test the power of his wishes. "I'd like to know what's under that hill there," he said, as he walked home from work. Suddenly, he was able to see into the earth, and he saw bones buried in the hill.

"Well!" he thought. "I have powers beyond those of other men." To test the power of his wishes further, he said, "I wish the owner of those bones would come alive, just as he was before he died." All of a sudden, the bones jumped up and turned into a lion that roared ferociously and chased him all the way home.

A Pot of Milk

A man was sitting with a big pot of milk in front of him. He was staring at the pot. Suddenly he said, "Wow!" Then he said, "Hah!" He never took his eyes off the pot. He said, "Ooh!" Then, "Ooh, Ooh, Ooh!" he exclaimed faster and louder as he waved his arms with great agitation. Suddenly, his hand hit the pot and it crashed to the floor and broke. All the milk spilled out. "Oh!" he shouted.

His wife had been watching him with increasing alarm, wondering if he was going crazy. "Are you okay?" she asked.

"I am now," he said.

"What happened? What are you so excited about?" she asked.

"I looked at that milk," he told her, "and I realized, if I make it into yogurt, I could sell it and buy twice as much milk. I could make more yogurt and sell it again. After six times, I could buy a goat. Then, if I have a goat, I can milk her every day. And if I have milk every day, I can make butter, too. I could sell the butter, and buy another goat. If we had two goats, next spring we'd have four! I'd have thousands of goats! Then I realized, I could shear my goats and get wool. With the wool, we could weave rugs, sell them in the market, then buy a big castle and then I'd… I got so excited, I broke the pot, and only when I felt the milk dripping on my feet did I come out of my castle."

Moses and the Shepherd

A shepherd was walking in the desert and talking to God. He sang, "Hey, where are you? I'd like to make a good soup for you. Where are you? I want to wash your hair, and wash your feet. I'd like to make your bed for you. Where are you? I'd like to bring you fresh milk."

Moses happened to be passing by, and he heard the young shepherd singing. "Who are you talking to?" he asked.

"Oh," said the young shepherd, "I'm talking to God."

"God? You don't ask God to come sit down, you don't ask to wash his hair and wash his feet and give him milk!"

"You don't?" asked the shepherd, timidly.

"Let me show you how to pray!" Moses said.

So he told the shepherd how to address God: "Dear Lord, have mercy," and all those beautiful prayers. Then he continued on his way.

The next day, God felt something was different. He missed the singing of his friend the shepherd.

Later, God spoke to Moses: "One of the most important jobs of a prophet is to nurture the relationship between people and myself. You created separation. Go back and see for yourself what's happened."

Moses went back and found the shepherd sitting on a rock. He was hitting his head with his fists, and saying, "I don't know what to say. I don't know how to talk to you. I don't know who you are, I don't know where you are."

Moses ran up to him and said, "Listen, forget about what I told you. I'll pray for God to forgive me, and please, you forgive me, too! What you were saying and doing when I first met you is a prayer dear to God's heart. Wash his hair, wash his feet, bring him milk!"

Wealth and Poverty

One day, a Teacher spoke to his students. "Wealth is an obstacle on the path to God." he said. "The poor have more possibilities."

The next day, he came to his students adorned with gold and diamonds and dressed in priceless clothing. When the students spoke to him, he ignored them, and leisurely examined his opulent jewelry.

The day after, he returned dressed in rags, holding one copper coin in his palm. When the students tried to speak to him, he stared intently at the coin, and then clenched it tightly in his hand.

Very few students understood this teaching. Not even his own son understood.

A few days later, he came back to his students. "Which me was richer?" he asked them.

"The first," they all said.

"Why so?" he asked. "Not every rich man is wealthy. Not every poor man is a pauper. Wealth and poverty refer to identification, not money. You could walk around with just one dollar to your name, and be too rich to think about anything else in the world. You could have millions, like King Solomon, and be totally non-identified. When he walked, he could hear and understand the language of the ants and the butterflies—that's how much receptivity and presence he had. Yet everything he owned was made of pure gold."

What Brought You to This Level?

Someone said to a Teacher, "Wherever you go, whatever you do, everyone benefits! What brought you to this level?"

"Only light exists," he answered. "And wherever there's a window, it will shine through."

This Is Mine

Two people were fighting with each other because they didn't agree on the boundary of their properties. Each kept saying, "This is mine! This is mine!"

An old man was passing by. The two men looked at each other and said, "We'll ask him." They grabbed the old man, and one of them shouted, "You see, this part is mine, and over there, that's mine, and…"

"No!" the other yelled. "This is mine, up to that stream, and beyond where the tree…"

"Wait," said the old man. "I don't know, and you don't know, and he doesn't know. Why don't we ask *her?*" He put his ear to the ground and tapped the earth gently. "Who is right?" he asked.

"They are both liars," the earth said. "*They* belong to me."

Late for Work

A group of workers used to catch a ride to and from work with their boss. One day, as they were driving back from lunch, one of the workers turned to the boss and asked, "Could we stop in that store and get something for dessert?" "We're already late for work," the boss answered, and kept driving.

The next day, they drove by the same store, and they were even more late for work. "Boy!" one of the workers said. "That place has such incredible cookies—I can smell 'em from here!" "Yeah," said the boss, "let's stop and get some!"

Candlelight

A great Master was a close friend of the King, who later became his student. One night they were sitting together. The Master stretched his arm toward a candle, quickly closed his hand near the flame, and then drew it back to himself. He opened it near his face, and stared at his palm intently. Then he did it again. And again and again. The King, who was watching quietly, finally got tired of it, and asked, "What are you doing?"

"I'm studying," answered the Master.

"Studying what?"

"Well, first of all I want to prove to myself that there *is* light. And second, that I don't have it."

BREEMA

Being

Right now

Everywhere

Every moment

Myself

Actually

About Breema

Breema, the art of being present, uses the transformational tools of Breema bodywork, Self-Breema exercises, and the Nine Principles of Harmony to support us to unify mind, feelings and body, and create harmony in our relationship to ourselves, to others, and to all life.

The aim of Breema is to bring us to a tangible experience of presence that becomes our foundation for a new dimension of health, consciousness, and Self-understanding.

Breema provides a unique approach to experiencing body-mind connection. It offers a profound understanding of the underlying unity of all life that is expressed in a dynamic and practical philosophy, the key to which is found in the Nine Principles of Harmony. Self-Breema exercises and Breema bodywork are living expressions of Breema's unifying philosophy.

BREEMA
The Nine Principles of Harmony

BODY COMFORTABLE

*When we look at the body, not as something separate,
but as an aspect of a unified whole,
there is no place for discomfort.*

NO EXTRA

To express our True nature, nothing extra is needed.

FIRMNESS AND GENTLENESS

*Real firmness is always gentle.
Real gentleness is always firm.
When we are present, we naturally
manifest firmness and gentleness simultaneously.*

FULL PARTICIPATION

*The most natural way of moving and living is with
full participation. Full participation is possible when body,
mind, and feelings are united in a common aim.*

MUTUAL SUPPORT

*The more our Being participates, the more we are
able to support life and recognize that Existence supports us.
Giving and receiving support
take place simultaneously.*

NO JUDGMENT

*The atmosphere of nonjudgment gives us a taste
of acceptance of ourselves as we are in the moment.
When we come to the present,
we are free from judgment.*

SINGLE MOMENT/SINGLE ACTIVITY

*Each moment is new, fresh, totally alive.
Each moment is an expression
of our True nature, complete by itself.*

NO HURRY/NO PAUSE

*In the natural rhythm of life energy,
there is no hurry and no pause.*

NO FORCE

*When we let go of assumptions of separation,
we let go of force.*

The Breema Center

Since 1980, the Breema Center has been presenting Breema's practical approach to harmony and Self-understanding. The world headquarters for practitioner and instructor certification and continuing education, the Center also gives classes, workshops, and intensives for students of all levels. People come from all over the world, attracted by Breema's philosophy, principles, bodywork, and exercises. Studying at the Center, they find essential support in creating a new, unified relationship between the body, mind, and feelings, and in bringing greater harmony and presence to their lives.

The Breema Center maintains an active relationship with Certified Breema Practitioners and Instructors.

Please visit our website for more information on Breema and an up-to-date international directory of Practitioners and Instructors, as well as listings of Breema classes and presentations worldwide.

THE BREEMA CENTER
Jon Schreiber, D.C., Director
6076 Claremont Avenue
Oakland, CA 94618

510-428-0937
email: center@breema.com
website: breema.com

The Breema Clinic

The Breema Clinic offers unique and deeply transformational support for health and well-being, centered around Breema bodywork and Self-Breema exercises, and integrated with a universal philosophy based on the Nine Principles of Harmony.

More than four decades of clinical experience have confirmed Breema's great value as a foundation for real health and as a catalyst for ongoing health improvement.

THE BREEMA CLINIC
Jon Schreiber, D.C., Director
6201 Florio Street
Oakland, CA 94618

510-428-1234
email: clinic@breema.com
website: breemahealth.com

Jon Schreiber

Jon Schreiber, D.C., director of the Breema Center and Breema Clinic in Oakland, California, has been teaching Breema in the U.S. and internationally since 1980. He has presented Breema to professional groups in the fields of medicine, psychology, bodywork, exercise, holistic health, and personal growth. In his active clinical practice, Dr. Schreiber uses Breema, Self-Breema, and the Nine Principles of Harmony to help his patients discover the real meaning of health.

In expressing his experience with Breema, Jon says, "Breema has been the most transformative influence in my life, and the source and foundation of my most meaningful experiences. Breema supports our essential desires—those we know of and those we haven't yet discovered—from the desire for more balance and harmony in our mind, feelings, and body, to the desire to relate harmoniously to other people, to the desire to take a step towards discovering and fulfilling the purpose and meaning of our life."

Books from The Breema Center
in print, eBook, & audio CD format
Available from local and online bookstores

BREEMA *and the Nine Principles of Harmony*   – by Jon Schreiber

Breema is universal and has great potential value to anyone with a sincere interest in Truth, because it's a practical road to Self-understanding. Breema's timeless principles are applicable to every situation in life, and they open us to the possibility of awakening to the essential unity of Existence in this very moment.

available in print, audio, and eBook format
print: hardcover, 168 pages,
     7" x 9", 81 photos • $25
audio: 2-CD set,
     read by Jon Schreiber • $20

Every Moment Is Eternal:
The Timeless Wisdom of Breema   – by Jon Schreiber

This book talks to our essential nature, because Truth already exists there. The more our essence is nurtured, the greater the chance that cracks may appear in our conditioned attitude towards life. Through these cracks, we may see things we haven't seen before, and nourish our essential desire for Self-understanding.

available in print and eBook format
print: hardcover, 208 pages, 4.5" x 6" • $15

Freedom Is in This Moment: *365 Insights for Daily Life*
– by Jon Schreiber

When you read these writings, you are filled up with an inner resonance, because their reality and meaning are in you as well as all around you. When you hear the Truth, you also hear it inside of yourself, in your very essence. The Truth is not something foreign. It's already part of you just because you exist!

available in print and eBook format
print: hardcover, 448 pages, 4.5" x 6" • $18.95

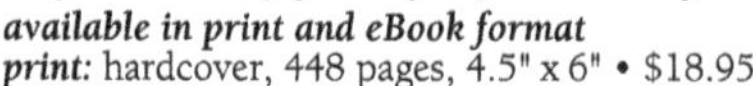

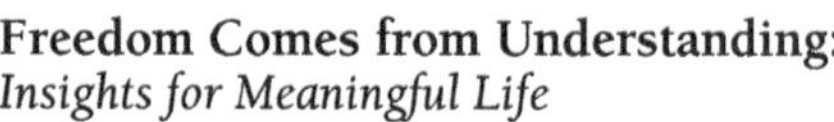

Freedom Comes from Understanding:
Insights for Meaningful Life

– by Jon Schreiber

How does Existence support you? By letting you know you belong. When you become conscious of your own existence, that Consciousness is the beginning of connection to your Timeless nature.

available in print, audio, and eBook format
print: hardcover, 172 pages, 5" x 7.25" • $18
audio: 2-CD set, read by Jon Schreiber • $20

The Four Relationships *and Other Essential Insights*

– by Jon Schreiber

The Four Relationships—our relationship to the body, our relationship to the outside world, our relationship to ourself, and our relationship to our True nature—provide a universal framework that enables us to usefully relate to the ingredients and issues of our life, and to find a meaningful posture and approach to the questions life places in front of us. This book explores the principles and philosophy of Breema.

available in print, audio, and eBook format
print: hardcover, 160 pages, 5" x 7.25" • $18
audio: 2-CD set, read by Jon Schreiber • $20

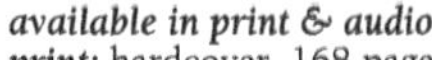

Waking Up to This Moment:
The Essential Meaning of Breema

– by Jon Schreiber

To the extent you are available at this moment, you are doing Breema. It's as simple as that. If you keep this direction clear for yourself and always work with it, you can come to a taste—the taste of being present. Instead of being drawn to the past or future, where you have been conditioned to live, it's possible to live your life with meaning and purpose in the present.

available in print & audio
print: hardcover, 168 pages, 7" x 9"
      60 color photos • $25
audio: 2-CD set, read by Jon Schreiber • $20

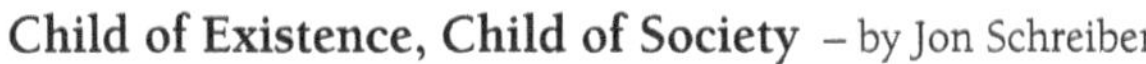

Child of Existence, Child of Society – by Jon Schreiber

There are two parts of us—the child of Existence and the child of society. The child of society is our acquired aspect, acquired from our education, from books, movies, radio, television, newspapers, the Internet. But we're more than that. We have also been given something by Existence. The child of Existence is our essential aspect, what we are in reality. The aim is to move from this outer part, this acquired part, towards the inner part—to find this essential part of ourself.

available in print & audio
print: hardcover, 208 pages, 5" x 7.25" • $18
audio: 2-CD set, read by Jon Schreiber • $20

Knowing and Being:
Breema and the Meaning of Your Life

– by Jon Schreiber

All moments of life are blessings, if we are present. We have to clearly see that the past is gone and the future is "elsewhere." But in this moment, we could be here, present. If there's something you need to do to repair the past, you still have to do it in this moment. In the present, there's always a chance to take a correct step for your life. If you need to prepare for the future, you can only do it in the present. That's where all your possibilities are.

available in print and eBook format
print: hardcover, 168 pages, 5.5" x 8.5" • $23.95

Your Home Is the Entire Cosmos: *The Wisdom of Breema*

– by Jon Schreiber

The desire to know, to be, and to understand is the essential heritage of being human. The most meaningful aspect of that desire is the desire to know oneself, to be oneself, and to understand oneself. Even though we don't know what "self" means, this gives us direction. It points towards *you*. In order to develop, you need to know yourself. To the extent you know yourself, you know other things, too.

print: hardcover, 192 pages, 5" x 7.25" • $18

In the Heart of the Moment: *Essential Poetry*

– collected by Jon Schreiber

These poems are doorways that open into the heart of Breema as a teaching for Self-understanding, and for understanding the world and our place and purpose in it.

print: hardcover, 112 pages, 5.25" x 8" • $15

In the Garden of All Possibilities: *Essential Poetry*

– collected by Jon Schreiber

These poems are meant to harmonize our inner aspect and bring it into equilibrium with Existence. Their vibration and sequence create a meaning. When you listen, you become an instrument. The poems tune you, and you resonate with their music.

print: hardcover, 112 pages, 5.25" x 8" • $15

The Taste of Being Present: *Essential Wisdom of Breema*

– by Jon Schreiber

You have to know where you are, wherever you are. Establish one "marker"—I am here in this moment. This first step is the most important thing in the world! Wherever you are, be where you are. Then, you can see the next step.

You study Breema in order to study yourself. You do Breema in order to be yourself. Being yourself means body, mind, and feelings functioning in the receptive state, receiving Conscious energy from your True nature. In those moments, you know yourself.

available in print & audio
print: hardcover, 172 pages, 5" x 7.25" • $18
audio: 2-CD set, read by Jon Schreiber • $20

Real Health Means Harmony with Existence:
The Art of Practicing Breema – by Jon Schreiber

You do Breema in order to become present, and by remaining present, to have presence, which is to receive the emanation of what *is*. In that, your *Being* participates. Understanding is a property of Being, and Being is in harmony with what is.

print: hardcover, 208 pages, 5" x 7.25" • $18

First You Have to *Be*:
The Nine Principles of Harmony in Breema and Life

– by Jon Schreiber

The purpose of Breema bodywork, Self-Breema exercises, and Breema's philosophy is to show us a new way of life—the way to be yourself in life, the way to participate in life, not in the reactive state, but in the active state, with body and mind together. From there, you have a chance to come to the receptive state—body, mind, and feelings together.

available in print & audio
print: hardcover, 192 pages, 5" x 7.25" • $18
audio: 2-CD set, read by Jon Schreiber • $20

Coming to Yourself: *The Art of Practicing Breema*

– by Jon Schreiber

To see things as they are, we have to *be* as we are. The taste of Being is received in the absence of thoughts, feelings, and sensations. When we receive that taste, we can see thoughts as thoughts, feelings as feelings, sensations as sensations. By not identifying with them, we enter into the awareness of our existence.

print: hardcover, 208 pages, 5" x 7.25" • $19

Seeing Things As They Really Are

– by Jon Schreiber

You can only see things as they really are when you see yourself as you are in relation to them. It means to see things as a part of your existence, not as separate phenomena. Existence is one unified whole—nothing separate exists. There is one life force, and it enters into everything that has been created. That means it also flows through you. When you are present, you experience it.

print: hardcover, 192 pages, 5" x 7.25" • $19

**Call 510.428.0937 to order Breema Center books & CDs,
or see our Bookstore at: breema.com
Check your favorite online stores for our print and eBooks.**